BOOMERANG

Our European Friends

1 Ireland	**4** Germany	**7** Luxembourg	**10** Spain
2 The UK	**5** Holland	**8** France	**11** Italy
3 Denmark	**6** Belgium	**9** Portugal	**12** Greece

CAMPS FOR YOUNG EUROPEANS

Are you 10-16?
Are you from an EEC country?
Do you want to practise a new language?
Do you want to learn about Europe?

Why not go to one of our camps
for young Europeans this summer?

For more information contact
your local EEC Commission.

Tasos 11 Greece
Greek and English

Lars 10 Denmark
Danish and English

Jean 16 Luxembourg
French and German

KOS - TIGAKI

Caroline 12 Belgium
French and Dutch

le mont sai

Mario 11 Portugal
Portuguese and English

Hans 10 Germany
German and Italian

Beatriz 16 Spain
Spanish and English

Simon 12 U.K.
English and French

Flavia 10 Italy
Italian and
German and
English.

Else 10 Holland
Dutch, English
and German

Patrick 13 Ireland
English

Charlotte 15 France
French and Spanish

Dieppe

L'ABSINTHE

Euro Information

LANGUAGE

In the twelve countries of the European Community people speak different languages. There are nine official languages: Danish, Dutch, English, French, German, Greek, Italian, Portuguese and Spanish. There are other languages but they are not official. For example, in Ireland some people speak Gaelic and in Spain some people speak Catalan, Gallego or Basque. Look at the map of the European Community on page 2. Each country is coloured according to the language the people speak. Which colour represents English and which colour represents Spanish?

HISTORY

The European Economic Community started on 25th March 1957. Now there are twelve countries, but at first there were only six: Belgium, Germany, France, Italy, Luxembourg and Holland. In 1973 three other countries joined: Denmark, Ireland and the U.K. Greece joined in 1979, and finally Spain and Portugal joined in 1981.

FLAG

This is the European flag. It is blue with a circle of yellow stars. There are twelve stars, one for each country in the Community.

THE PEOPLE

The people of the European Community can live and work in any of the countries of the Community. They can also take things from one country to another. Which country would you like to live in?

Goodies and Baddies

1 tall	**3** fat	**5** face	**7** moustache	**9** straight
2 short	**4** thin	**6** beard	**8** hair	**10** curly

Who's Who?

Obelix

Frankenstein

He's big and very fat. He's got a big nose, a big mouth and small eyes. He's got long red hair and a big moustache. He can eat a big pig in one minute.

Tarzan

He's tall and strong. He's got long hair and blue eyes. He can swim very fast and run through the jungle.

He's very tall and very strong. His head is very big with a flat top and his hair is very short. He's got small eyes, a big mouth, and a big nose. His arms are very long, and his feet are very big. He can break doors.

He's tall and strong. He's got a nice face and short straight black hair. He can fly, and he can jump over a house.

Superman

7

The Story of Dracula

Dracula is tall and thin with short black hair. He wears black trousers, a white shirt and a black **cape** with a red lining.

He's got a thin, white face, and very big black and red eyes.

His mouth is normal, but when he opens it you can see two very big and horrible **fangs**.

He lives in a **castle** in Transylvania, which is in Rumania.

He sleeps during the **day** in his coffin in his grave.

He flies about at **night**.

He is **afraid** of three things: the light, crucifixes and garlic.

He loves **blood**.

He's a very bad **vampire**.

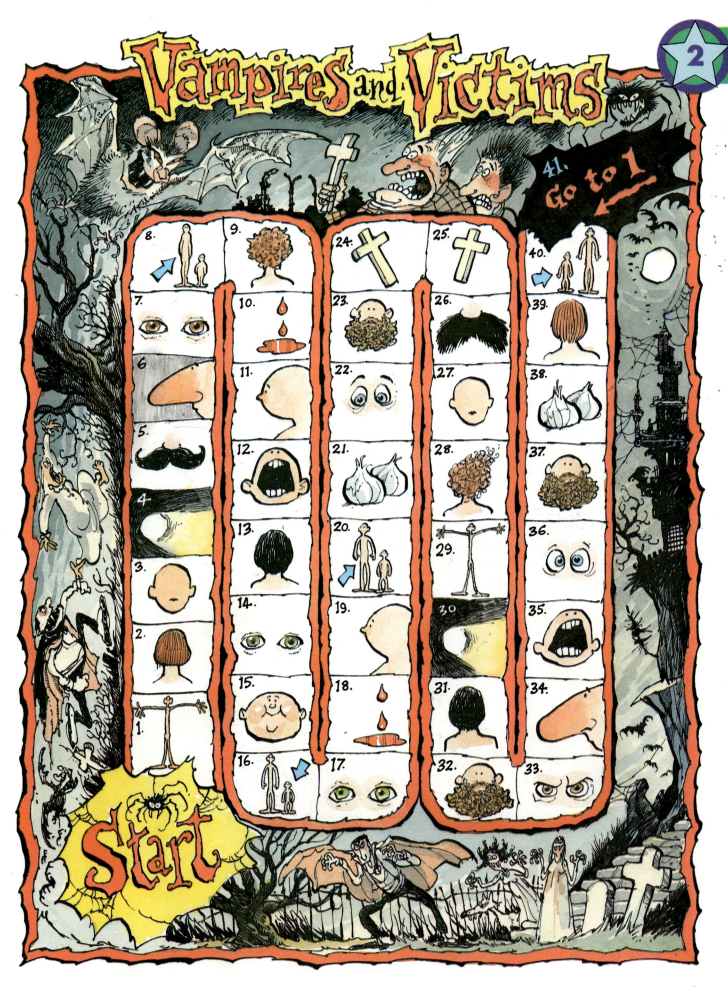

Helping at Home

1. wash the dishes
2. tidy your bedroom
3. clean the bathroom
4. cook the dinner
5. water the plants
6. sweep the floor
7. feed the cat
8. walk the dog
9. make your bed
10. lay the table

The Story of Andrello

THE ROBOT SONG

I'm a robot, I'm a robot.
I lay the table.
I'm a robot, I'm a robot.

I cook the dinner.
I feed the cat,
I clean the bathroom,
I walk the dog,
I tidy the bedroom,
I make the bed,
I sweep the floor.
When you come home
I open the door.

FLASH is VERY HAPPY

This is my robot. It is very very big and fat. It has got no hair. It tidies the bedroom and lays the table in the morning. In the afternoon it waters the plants and sweeps the floors.

Bimbo

Simon (age 12)

BIMBO

BIMBO K2-3000

My robot is a very clever robot. It makes the beds, walks the dog, washes the dishes and cleans the bathroom. My robot is thin. It has got short straight hair (and pink!).

Wally

Angie (age 10)

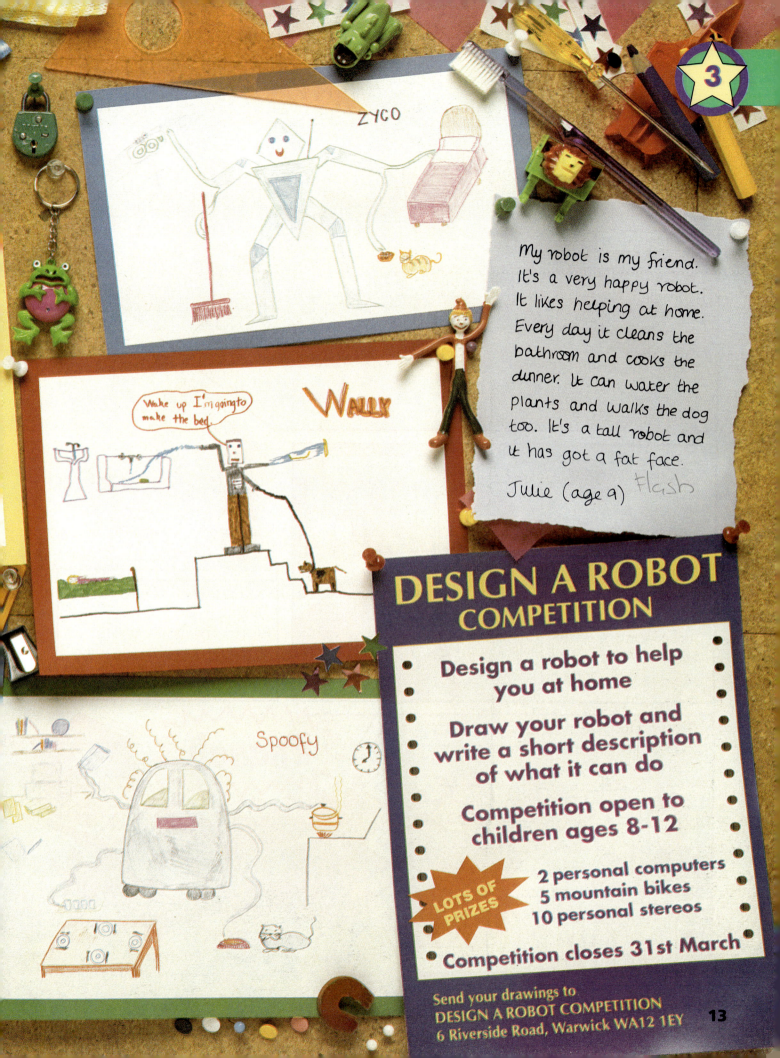

ZYCO

My robot is my friend.
It's a very happy robot.
It likes helping at home.
Every day it cleans the
bathroom and cooks the
dinner. It can water the
plants and walks the dog
too. It's a tall robot and
it has got a fat face.

Julie (age 9)   Flash

Wake up I'm going to
make the bed.

WALLY

Spoofy

DESIGN A ROBOT
COMPETITION

**Design a robot to help
you at home**

**Draw your robot and
write a short description
of what it can do**

**Competition open to
children ages 8-12**

LOTS OF
PRIZES

2 personal computers
5 mountain bikes
10 personal stereos

Competition closes 31st March

Send your drawings to:
DESIGN A ROBOT COMPETITION
6 Riverside Road, Warwick WA12 1EY

PROFESSOR WONG GOES NORTH

1 This is Apple Street in Manchester. Manchester is in the north of England. Can you see Wong's Takeaway? It has got a blue door. People buy a Chinese lunch or supper or even breakfast in Wong's Takeaway and take it away to eat.

2 Oh look! Here are Brenda and Eddie. They are friends. They like Chinese food and they like Professor Wong. On Fridays they go to Wong's Takeaway in the evening to buy their supper and to speak to Professor Wong.

Hello, Professor Wong!

Good evening, Brenda. Good evening, Eddie. Look what I've got!

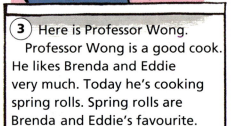

3 Here is Professor Wong. Professor Wong is a good cook. He likes Brenda and Eddie very much. Today he's cooking spring rolls. Spring rolls are Brenda and Eddie's favourite.

4 What's that?!! Professor Wong drops a spring roll and the shop begins to move. Oh dear! What's happening?

5 *Whaaa!!*

Oooooooops !!!!!

Off they go!!! Goodbye, Apple Street. Goodbye, Manchester. Oh, where are they going?!

6 This is Professor Wong. He's from China. He's very good and very clever. He can control animals with his eyes and go at 400 kilometres an hour on his magic rollerskates. He can cook lovely Chinese food and he can speak twelve languages (he can do other things too, but that's a secret).

And this is Professor Wong's dog. His name is Marmaduke.

7 This is the Crazton Family. They are very, very, very bad!! The Crazton Family live on Planet Crazton. They get up at 8 o'clock in the morning. They have snake hamburgers for breakfast, and spider pizzas for lunch. In the evening they have shark salad.

They want to control the Earth. They hate Professor Wong.

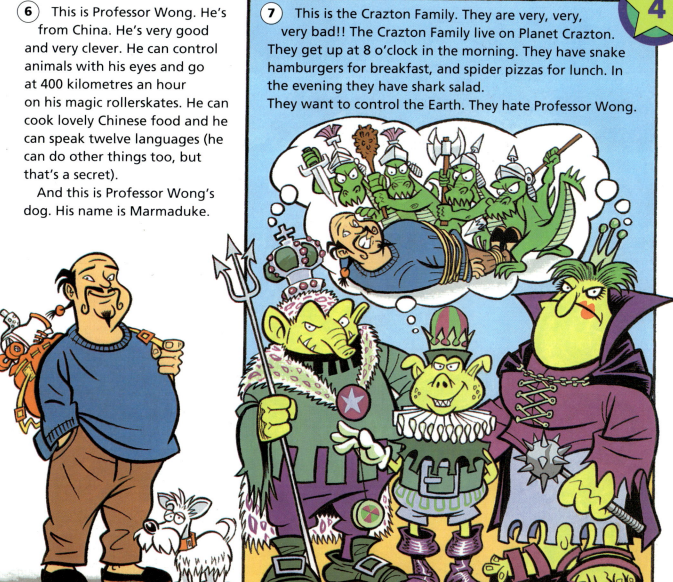

8 The Grippies are the soldiers of the Crazton Family. They are very, very bad. They go to the Earth to do bad things.

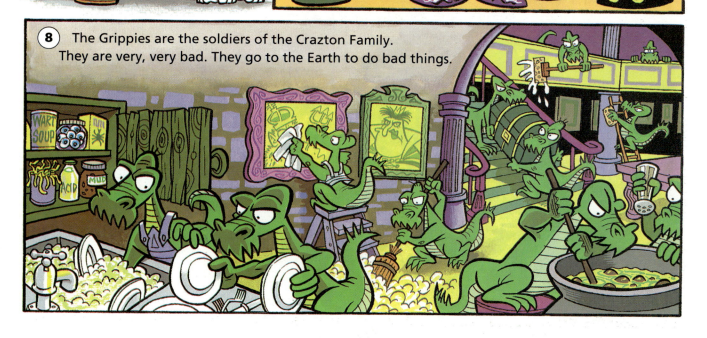

I Saw Three Ships Come Sailing in

I saw three ships come sailing in,
On Christmas Day, on Christmas Day.
I saw three ships come sailing in,
On Christmas Day in the morning.

And what was in those ships all three,
On Christmas Day, on Christmas Day?
And what was in those ships all three,
On Christmas Day in the morning?

The Virgin Mary and Christ were there,
On Christmas Day, on Christmas Day.
The Virgin Mary and Christ were there,
On Christmas Day in the morning.

And all the bells on earth shall ring,
On Christmas Day, on Christmas Day.
And all the bells on earth shall ring,
On Christmas Day in the morning.

And all the angels in heaven shall sing,
On Christmas Day, on Christmas Day.
And all the angels in heaven shall sing,
On Christmas Day in the morning.

Christmas Figure Cards

1 Fold the piece of paper in half.

2 Draw half a picture on the folded line.

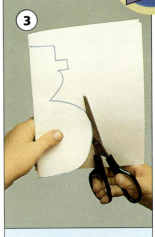

3 Cut out your picture.

4 Unfold the paper. Now you can see the whole figure!

5 Decorate your figure.

6 Here are some other things you could make.

7 Write your message on the back.

21

The Time

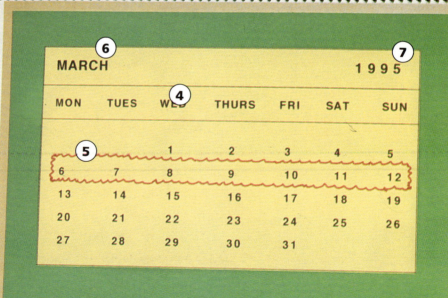

MARCH						1995
MON	TUES	WED	THURS	FRI	SAT	SUN
		1	2	3	4	5
6	7	8	9	10	11	12
13	14	15	16	17	18	19
20	21	22	23	24	25	26
27	28	29	30	31		

1 second
2 minute
3 hour
4 day
5 week
6 month
7 year
8 watch
9 clock
10 calendar

24

Make a clock.

1 Draw a circle on a piece of card and cut it out.

2 Use the rest of the card to make a minute hand and an hour hand. Cut the minute hand the same as the diameter of the circle. Cut the hour hand a little shorter.

3 Label your clock like this to help you tell the time.

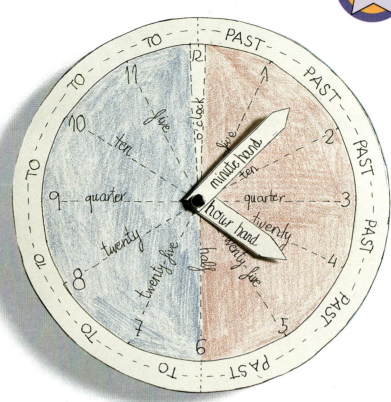

What's the time, Mr Wolf?

A Game

What's the time, Mr Wolf?
Eight o'clock.
What's the time, Mr Wolf?
Eleven o'clock.
What's the time, Mr Wolf?
Half past twelve.
What's the time, Mr Wolf?
Quarter to one.
What's the time, Mr Wolf
Quarter past one.
What's the time, Mr Wolf
Twenty five past one.
What's the time, Mr Wolf?
Dinner time!

Can you find the kidnapped girl?

At every junction solve
the clue and you will find
the treasure!

MURDOCH POINT

BLUE MOUNTAIN

SMUGGLERS BAY

The hours in 7 days.

The feet of 9 elephants plus the days of November.

The letters in the alphabet plus the syllables in 3

168

228

148

48

28 29

30

35

62

66

31

CLARKS HARBOUR

The minutes from half past two to quarter to nine.

The letters in [turtle] multiplied by the days in March.

375

340

295

240

The months in a year multiplied by 5.

186

248 217

THE OLD LIGHTHOUSE

48

60

72 80

52 32

The days of 3 years.

2080 1095

704

860

53

The complete weeks in a year.

TOMS TAVERN

BLACK MOUNTAIN

plus	+
minus	−
divided by	÷
multiplied by	x

FLUME LIGHTHOUSE

The minutes from ten to six to five past seven.

HUNTERS ROCKS

780

1440 1780 1780 44 56

52 56

26 36

The legs of 13 tables.

75

56

95

19 14

18 21

The minutes in one day.

The days of the week plus your eyes and toes.

The grammes in a kilogramme minus the letters in

The hands of a teacher, 9 boys and 11 girls.

THE NEW LIGHTHOUSE

992

993 75 92

19

90 80

The feet of 16 rabbits divided by the legs of a boy.

78

87

72

The millimetres in a centimetre multiplied by the letters in

30

WILLIAM POINT

12

60 30 124 16

The legs of a centipede minus the eyes of 11 frogs.

15

The seconds in a minute divided by your ears.

(1) teeth	(3) chew	(5) vegetables	(7) fizzy drinks	(9) milk
(2) bite	(4) fruit	(6) sweets	(8) ice-creams	(10) dessert

Animals and food

horse 1

human 2

mouse 3

shark 4

nuts and seeds

grass

sharp teeth

long sharp teeth

OUR BILLY

I like sweets and chocolate.
I like fizzy drinks.
I eat biscuits every day,
And ice-cream twice a week.

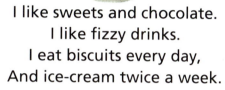

I never eat fruit or vegetables.
I don't like fish or meat,
Though sometimes I eat a hamburger
With lots of lovely chips.

Oh dear! Oh dear! What is that noise?
What is that dreadful drill?
I fear our Billy's in great pain.
He's in the dentist's chair again!

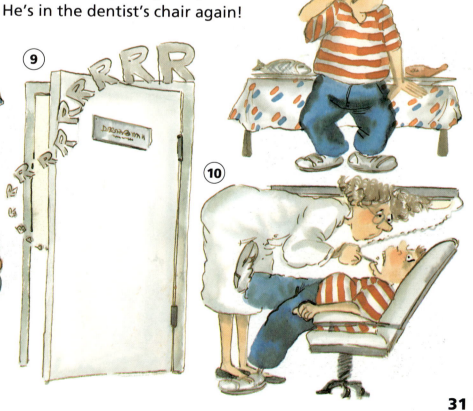

1 the Earth
2 ocean
3 sea
4 island
5 peninsula
6 continent
7 desert
8 high
9 long
10 small

Professor Huggins at home

About the Earth

A.

Here it is warm and sunny in June, July and August, and cold and snowy in December, January and February.

C.

Here there is a very big desert. It is very hot and very sunny. There is no water except in oases.

THE SAHARA DESERT

THE EQUATOR

E.

There is water in nearly 3/4 of the Earth. The oceans are connected. You can go round the world on a boat and not see one country!

B.

There is land in 1/4 of the Earth.
Most of the land is north of the Equator.

D.

This is the Equator.
Here it is very hot and very rainy.
There are jungles with beautiful animals
and plants.

F.

This is the South Pole.
Here it is very, very, very cold!
Penguins, seals and scientists live here.

CONTINENTS

OCEANS

Pacific Ocean 179,000,000 km²

Atlantic Ocean 92,040,000 km²

Indian Ocean 74,900,000 km²

Arctic Ocean
14,060,000 km²

RIVERS

Nile (Africa) 6,671km

Amason-Ucayali (S.America) 6,280km

Mississippi-Missouri (S. America) 5,971km

Yangtse-Kiang (Asia) 5,500km

0   100   200   300   400   500   600

MOUNTAINS

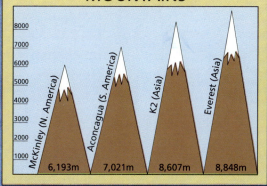

McKinley (N. America) 6,193m
Aconcagua (S. America) 7,021m
K2 (Asia) 8,607m
Everest (Asia) 8,848m

PROFESSOR WONG IN ANCIENT ROME

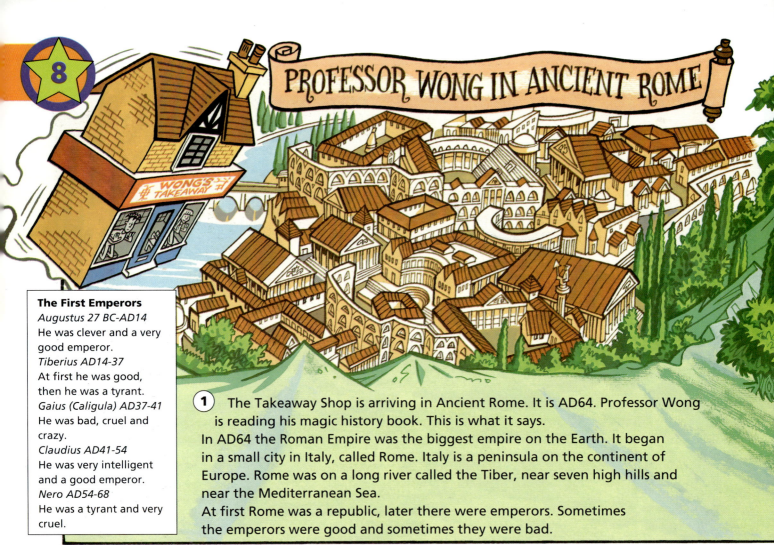

The First Emperors
Augustus 27 BC-AD14
He was clever and a very good emperor.
Tiberius AD14-37
At first he was good, then he was a tyrant.
Gaius (Caligula) AD37-41
He was bad, cruel and crazy.
Claudius AD41-54
He was very intelligent and a good emperor.
Nero AD54-68
He was a tyrant and very cruel.

1 The Takeaway Shop is arriving in Ancient Rome. It is AD64. Professor Wong is reading his magic history book. This is what it says.

In AD64 the Roman Empire was the biggest empire on the Earth. It began in a small city in Italy, called Rome. Italy is a peninsula on the continent of Europe. Rome was on a long river called the Tiber, near seven high hills and near the Mediterranean Sea.

At first Rome was a republic, later there were emperors. Sometimes the emperors were good and sometimes they were bad.

2 This is the Roman school where Professor Wong, Eddie and Brenda landed.
A These were Roman numbers from one to ten.
B This was for counting and doing sums.
C These were for writing on. There was no paper.
D This was a Roman pen and rubber. There were no pencils, or felt tips, or crayons.
E These were Roman books.
F And this was a Roman calendar.

③ This is Persius. He is the teacher. He's the best teacher in Rome. He is Greek. He is from the island of Crete. He is a slave. He likes Rome and he likes the Romans, but he doesn't like the emperor Nero. He teaches the children that Nero is a tyrant. Look at the window. Nero's spies are watching Persius.

④ Persius can speak Latin. Professor Wong can speak Latin too!

SALVE! QUIS ES TU?

SALVE! EGO SUM PROFESSOR WONG.

⑤ With Professor Wong's magic bracelet Persius can speak to Eddie and Brenda in English.

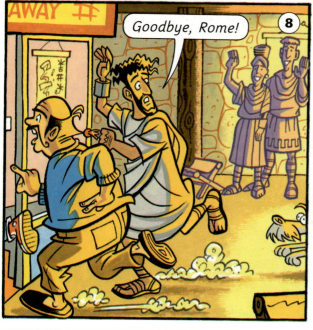

Freetime Fun

(1) went	(3) read	(5) wrote	(7) ate	(9) helped
(2) played	(4) watched	(6) rode	(8) drank	(10) drew

44

The Vikings

The Vikings were from Scandinavia. They lived from 800-1100.

The Vikings were very violent. In summer they went on raids. They went to countries in western Europe: England, Scotland, Ireland and France. They killed the people and stole the treasure.

They went in long boats made of wood. The Vikings loved their boats. There were about thirty men in each boat.

The Vikings lived in long houses. There was one big room which was the living room, the kitchen and the bedroom all in one. There was one very little window. The slaves helped with the cooking and cleaning.

In winter it was very cold and the Vikings stayed at home. They rode horses and went swimming. They watched horses fight. They played a ball game and a board game.

The Vikings ate lots of fish. They also ate meat. Sometimes they even ate it raw. They made sausages from blood and meat. They drank beer.

The Vikings wrote in runes, the letters of the Viking alphabet. They wrote on rocks. People who wrote and read runes were very important.

Last Weekend

On Saturday morning I helped my mum and dad to tidy the house. We had lunch at home and in the afternoon we went to my granny's house. My cousins were there too. It was a sunny day and we all played in the garden. It was my little cousin's birthday, he was five. He had a big cake. We ate it all!

On Saturday morning it was rainy so we stayed at home. I drew some pictures and then played computer games with my brother. We ate fish and chips for lunch and ice-cream for dessert. In the afternoon it was still rainy. I read some comics and my brother read a book about Nero. Then we watched T.V. I helped my mum make supper and went to bed at half past nine.

On Saturday morning I went to the park with my dad and my sister. I rode my bike and played football with my friends. Then we went home and ate an enormous lunch. After lunch we played at home, and in the evening I went to a friend's house. We watched a video and ate a pizza and drank fizzy drinks. I went to bed very late. At eleven o'clock.

THE JONESES AT THE SAFARI PARK

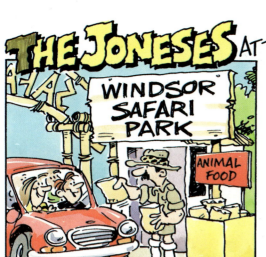

1	sheriff	**3**	outlaw	**5**	Indian	**7**	hungry	**9**	tired
2	a horse	**4**	gun	**6**	gold	**8**	thirsty	**10**	ill

The Story of Big Bad Bob

Big Bad Bob was the biggest and the strongest outlaw in the West.

One sunny morning he rode into Abilene. In Abilene there was a very prosperous bank.

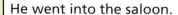

He went into the saloon.

The famous sheriff of Abilene, Bill Hickock, went into the saloon.

Big Bad Bob's hand went to his gun.

The sheriff wasn't afraid.

Bob pulled out his gun but the sheriff was first.

Big Bad Bob was buried outside Abilene and all the people were happy, especially the bank manager!!

THE PIONEER TRAIL

finish	41 	40 Oh no! Outlaws! Give them your gold.	39 Friends come to help you on your farm.	38 You find some gold in a river.	37 7 p.m.	36
29	30 Oh no! Outlaws! Give them your gold.	31 Friends come to help you on your farm.	32 2 p.m.	33 You find some gold in a river.	34	35
28	27 5 p.m.	26 It's very cold! −40	25 You lose your gun.	24 Buffalo Bill offers to help you.	23	22
15 Buffalo Bill offers to help you.	16	17	18 5 p.m.	19	20 You lose your gun.	21 It's very cold! −40
14 A rattlesnake bites you! You're ill! Wait for the doctor.	13	12 7 p.m.	11	10 5 p.m.	9 An Indian gives you some blankets.	8 Buffalo! Good! There is food for a week.
Start	2	3 An Indian gives you some blankets.	4 Buffalo! Good! There is food for a week.	5 A rattlesnake bites you! You're ill! Wait for the doctor.	6	7

OREGON · THE ROCKY MOUNTAINS · THE GREAT PLAINS

KEY

go forward three squares

go back three squares

go forward four squares

go back four squares

go back four squares

go forward three squares

go forward four squares

blankets

go back three squares

go forward four squares

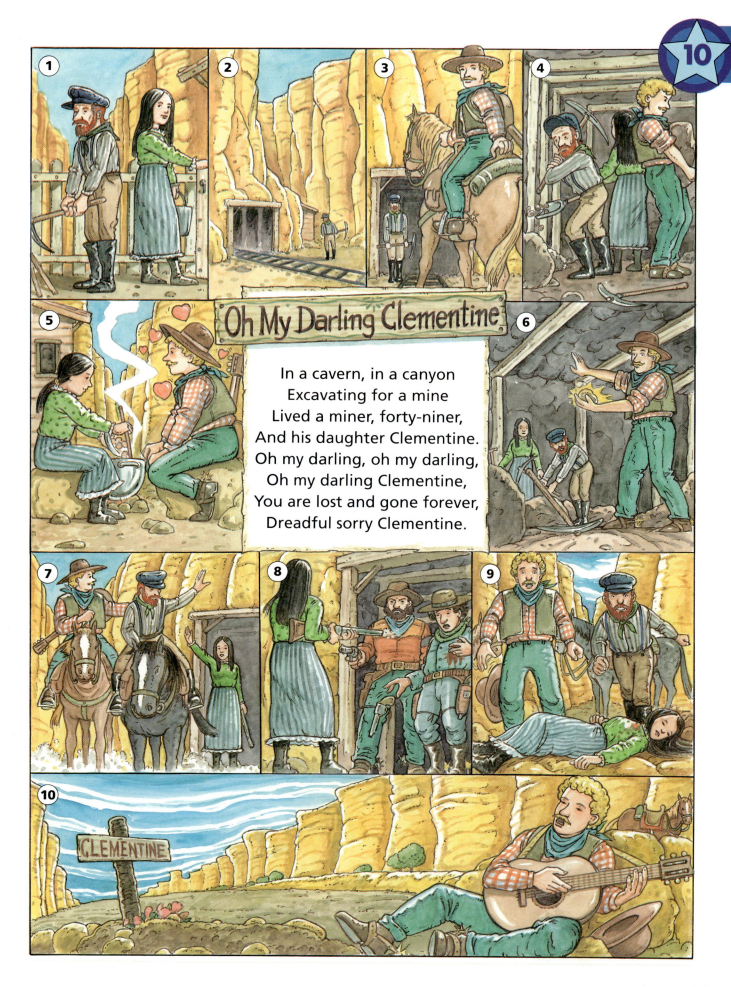

Oh My Darling Clementine

In a cavern, in a canyon
Excavating for a mine
Lived a miner, forty-niner,
And his daughter Clementine.
Oh my darling, oh my darling,
Oh my darling Clementine,
You are lost and gone forever,
Dreadful sorry Clementine.

1 crossed		**3** walked		**5** up		**7** over		**9** around	
2 sailed		**4** discovered		**6** down		**8** under		**10** through	

Ten Little Indians

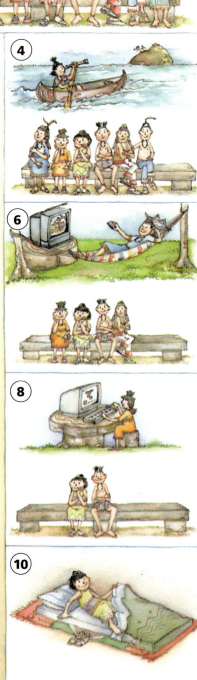

Ten little Indians sat in a row,
One crossed a desert,
And then there were nine.
Nine little Indians sat in a row,
One hunted buffalo,
And then there were eight.
Eight little Indians sat in a row,
One walked to Spain,
And then there were seven.
Seven little Indians sat in a row,
One discovered an island,
And then there were six.
Six little Indians sat in a row,
One sailed round the Earth,
And then there were five.
Five little Indians sat in a row,
One watched the TV,
And then there were four.
Four little Indians sat in a row
One helped his mum,
And then there were three.
Three little Indians sat in a row,
One played computer games,
And then there were two.
Two little Indians sat in a row,
One wanted an ice-cream,
And then there was one.
One little Indian sat all alone.
Well, he decided to go to bed,
And then there were none!

11

ACROSS THE DESERT AND THROUGH THE JUNGLE

I discovered the river.

I rode around the mountain.

I walked over the bridge.

I discovered the lake.

I went through the jungle.

I went around the jungle.

I sailed over the lake.

I walked under the bridge.

I discovered the mountain.

1. Do you remember that poor Marmaduke was captured in Rome by the Grippies? Professor Wong was very sad! Eddie and Brenda were very sad too!

2. They went back to Manchester. Professor Wong watched his magic television to try to find Marmaduke.

3. Brenda and Eddie went with Persius to explore Manchester. Professor Wong didn't want to go. He wanted to watch his magic television and find Marmaduke.

4. They walked down the road. "AAAAAH!!" shouted Persius "What's that?!!" He was very afraid. "That's a bus!" said Brenda. They went past a bus station, a school, a park and a police station. "What's that?" said Persius. "It's a police station" said Eddie. "The police help people and arrest criminals."

5. They went to the City hall. Persius said good morning to the mayor. They went to a sports centre and they played basketball with some friends of Brenda and Eddie's.

6 They went to the zoo and rode on some elephants. They went to a funfair and went for a ride on The Big Dipper.

7 They went to a museum and saw some dinosaurs. Eddie read to them about the Tyrannosaurus, which was a big carnivorous dinosaur. Persius drew a picture of a Triceratops. Triceratops was a herbivorous dinosaur.

This was the biggest carnivorous dinosaur.

Ugh!

8 They were all very hungry and thirsty. They went to a café. Persius ate some ice-cream and drank a fizzy drink. He didn't like the fizzy drink very much, but he liked the ice-cream!!

Ugh!!!

Joe's Cafe

9 Brenda, Eddie and Persius went to find Professor Wong. Professor Wong was very excited.

Come on ... Come on! I know where Marmaduke is. He's on Planet Crazton!!

57

PROFESSOR WONG ON PLANET CRAZTON

58

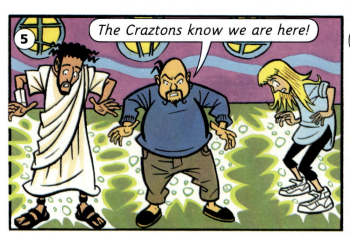